# Introduction

Vietnam possesses vast untapped mineral resources in the form of rare earth elements (REEs), which in Vietnam are found together with naturally occurring radioactive materials (NORMs) including uranium. Vietnam has a stated national strategic goal of increased exploration and exploitation of mineral resources "to assure socio-economic sustainable development, national defense and [national] security."[1] Vietnam also has an ambitious plan to establish a domestic nuclear power-generating capability, intending to construct 13 nuclear power plants beginning in 2014, to provide 10.1% of total domestic power generation by 2030.[2] China's near-monopolistic domination of the present world supply of REEs – a position which China uses to advantage through a system of export quotas that (whether by design or not) artificially maintain higher prices – has led some, including the U.S. Congress, to question whether Chinese control of REEs does not pose a strategic threat to the United States.[3] As REEs are necessary to many key components of defense-related applications – such as guidance and control systems for the Predator drone and electric motors in the F-35 Joint Strike Fighter – locating additional sources would alleviate these concerns. Due to the specific qualities of Vietnam's REE ore bodies, Vietnam may be an excellent source of alternate supply for the REEs the United States and her allies are seeking. Processing the ore containing these elements could – through reprocessing – also yield uranium oxides suitable for further processing into fuel. This could in turn help Vietnam achieve its nuclear power-generation goals. The United States and Vietnam would do well to pursue a collaborative

---

[1] The National Assembly of the Socialist Republic of Vietnam, *Law No. 60/2010/QH12 of November 17, 2010 on Mineral Law (2010 Mineral Law),* Article 3(1).

[2] The Prime Minister of the Socialist Republic of Vietnam, *Decision No. 1208/QD-TTg of July 21, 2011 on Approval of the National Master Plan for Power Development for the 2011-2020 Period with Vision to 2030 (Master Power Plan VII),* Article 1(3)(a).

[3] U.S. Library of Congress, Congressional Research Service. *Rare Earth Elements in National Defense: Background, Oversight Issues, and Options for Congress,* 27.

effort on the development and exploitation of Vietnamese REE deposits and their

concomitant NORM ores, to their mutual benefit.

## Rare Earth Elements – An Overview

Rare earth elements are a group of the 15 elements of the Lanthanide series. Scandium and yttrium are commonly added to this group, as they have similar chemical properties and frequently occur together in mineral formations with the Lanthanide metals, making a total of 17 elements (see Figure 1).[4] REEs are frequently classed as Light (L) or Heavy (H)

**Figure 1.** Periodic table of the elements showing the 15 rare earth elements of the Lanthanide series, plus yttrium and scandium.

**Source:** Periodic table from http://chemistry.about.com, modified by the author.

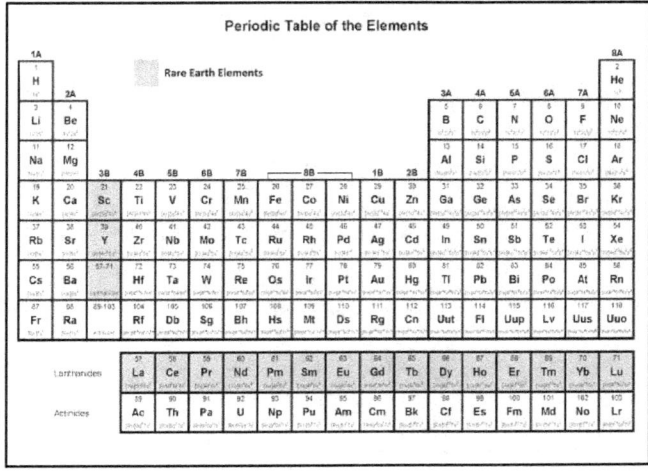

REEs. HREEs include yttrium and the series of eight elements from gadolinium through

lutetium.[5] Despite being called "rare," these elements are in fact relatively common in the

Earth's crust. With the exception of promethium, all the REEs are more abundant than both

silver and gold, while yttrium is actually three times more abundant than lead.[6] Unlike gold

or lead however, REEs do not naturally occur in pure metallic form, and are found only as

compounds in carbonate, phosphate, silicate, or oxide form; of these, only rare earth oxides

(REOs) have significant commercial value, and these are generally found in very low

concentrations. Furthermore, the specific nuclear and geochemical properties of the HREEs

---

[4] U.S. Department of the Interior, U.S. Geological Survey. *2011 Minerals Yearbook: Rare Earths [Advance Release]*, 60.1.
[5] U.S. Library of Congress, Congressional Research Service. *Rare Earth Elements: The Global Supply Chain*, 2.
[6] U.S. Environmental Protection Agency, *Rare Earth Elements: A Review of Production, Processing, Recycling, and Associated Environmental Issues*, 2-2.

tend to prevent concentrations of these heavier elements from forming at all; as a result, "deposits containing relatively high grades of the scarcer and more valuable heavy REE…and europium are particularly desirable."[7] The scarcity of ore bodies containing high concentrations (>2% by weight) of REOs – particularly the HREEs – and the difficulty of isolating the elements in metallic form from these oxides, has limited global supply to a few sources, and deservedly earns them the sobriquet "rare."[8]

In addition to this relative geologic scarcity, a complicating factor is that the three most common mineral ore sources of REOs – bastnäsite, monazite, and xenotime – typically occur together with concentrations of NORMs as high as 10% by weight, resulting in high background radioactivity at the deposit sites, as well as presenting significant challenges in processing the ores to extract REEs.[9]

The chief economic value of REEs has only been significantly uncovered in the last quarter-century. Their unique chemical, nuclear, and magnetic properties have made them essential in everything from computers to wind turbines, high-capacity rechargeable batteries, and electric vehicles. Europium, for example, provides the red color in liquid-crystal displays, while high-strength REE magnets made from neodymium are a key component in both flash-drive and electric vehicle technologies.[10] There are also critical applications pertinent to national defense, including: targeting and weapon systems (yttrium, europium, terbium); satellite and communications systems, including advanced radar and sonar systems (yttrium, lanthanum, neodymium, europium, lutetium); missile guidance and

---

[7] U.S. Department of the Interior, *U.S. Geological Survey Fact Sheet 087-02: Rare Earth Elements – Critical Resources for High Technology*, 3.
[8] U.S. Environmental Protection Agency, *Rare Earth Elements: A Review of Production, Processing, Recycling, and Associated Environmental Issues*, 2-1.
[9] Pillai, P.M.B., "Naturally Occurring Radioactive Material (NORM) in the Extraction and Processing of Rare Earths," 1.
[10] U.S. Department of the Interior, *U.S. Geological Survey Fact Sheet 087-02: Rare Earth Elements – Critical Resources for High Technology*, 2.

control systems (praseodymium, samarium, terbium, dysprosium); as well as electric motors and jet engines (neodymium, praseodymium, samarium, terbium, dysprosium).[11]

## Supply Issues – China's Role

Given the wide variety of high-tech applications to which REEs are essential, global demand for these elements has been growing rapidly in recent years, and is expected to increase still more in the near future. In 2010, world demand was 136,100 tons,[12] while estimates for total demand by 2015 range from 185,000 tons to 210,000 tons.[13] China has been able to supply most of the world's required REEs over the past 20 years due to herculean efforts to increase their output of these resources. Chinese production of REEs rose some 450% over the course of the 1990s, and another 77% over the decade of the 2000s; at the same time, output by other countries declined precipitously, dropping over 93% in the same period.[14] As a result, China now dominates the global market for REEs, producing 97% of REOs in 2011, the latest year for which full data is available (see Figure 2).

**Figure 2.** Global REO production, 1960-2011.
**Source:** Tse, Pui-Kwan. *China's Rare-Earth Industry: U.S. Geological Survey Open-File Report 2011–1042*, 3.

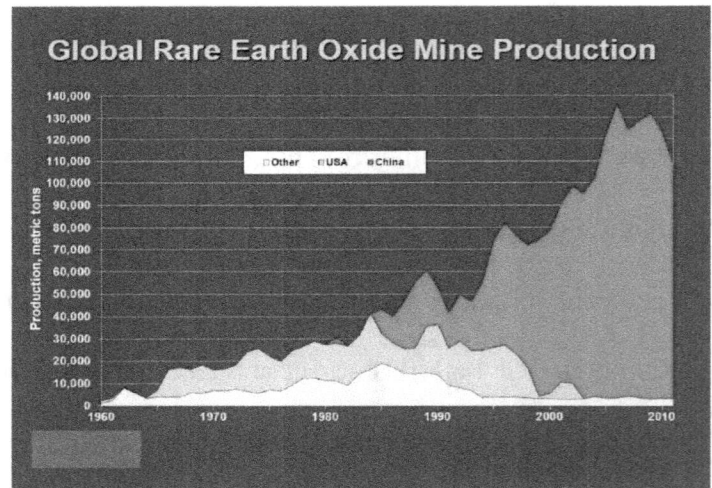

---

[11] U.S. Environmental Protection Agency, *Rare Earth Elements: A Review of Production, Processing, Recycling, and Associated Environmental Issues*, 2-6; U.S. Library of Congress, Congressional Research Service. *Rare Earth Elements: The Global Supply Chain*, 2; U.S. Library of Congress, *Rare Earth Elements in National Defense: Background, Oversight Issues, and Options for Congress*, 9-11.

[12] All references in this paper to a "ton" refer to a metric ton, equal to 2,204 lbs.

[13] Data from U.S. Library of Congress, Congressional Research Service. *Rare Earth Elements: The Global Supply Chain*, 4.

[14] Tse, Pui-Kwan. *China's Rare-Earth Industry: U.S. Geological Survey Open-File Report 2011–1042*, 2.

The Chinese government has increasingly recognized the strategic value of their position as the preeminent global supplier of REOs, and since 2000 has manipulated the market through a series of export quotas. In the eight years since 2005, this quota system has steadily reduced the availability of Chinese REOs to the global market by more than 50% (see Figure 3).[15] The sharpest quota reduction came in 2010, and was further exacerbated in September of that year when China temporarily halted shipments of all REOs to Japan following a flare-up of tensions over the Senkaku islands. Although the embargo was lifted after just two months, quotas have remained within 3% of the 2010 level ever since, prompting the United States, together with the European Union and Japan, to file a challenge with the World Trade Organization against China's REO export restrictions in March 2012. To date, China has maintained that these quota reductions were not an attempt to exert their monopolistic control of the market by artificially restricting supply in the interest of higher commodity prices, but were rather "motivated by environmental concerns."[16]

**Figure 3.** Chinese REO Export Quotas 2000-2013. **Source:** Chart created by author.

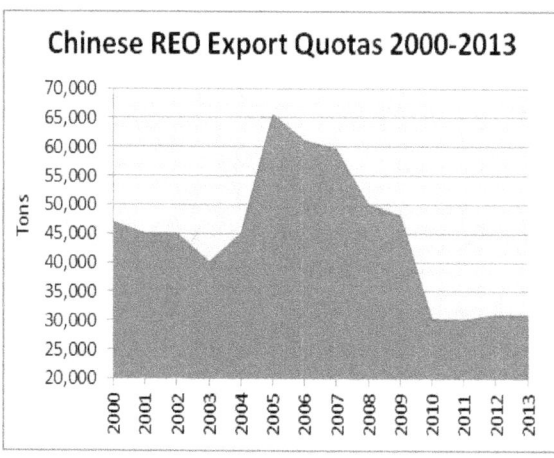

China's actions have had a drastic result on the global metals marketplace, with prices/kg for most REOs up 182% by the end of 2011, as compared to 2010.[17] While this

---

[15] Data for chart in Figure 3 compiled from three sources: Tse, Pui-Kwan. *China's Rare-Earth Industry: U.S. Geological Survey Open-File Report 2011–1042,* 4; Areddy, James T. and Chuin-Wei Yap. "China Raises Rare-Earth Export Quota." *The Wall Street Journal,* August 22, 2012; Kosich, Dorothy. "China Announces Second REE Quota for 2013." *Mineweb,* July 2, 2013.

[16] "Obama Announces WTO Case Against China over Rare Earths." *CNN,* March 13, 2012.

[17] U.S. Department of the Interior, U.S. Geological Survey. *2011 Minerals Yearbook: Rare Earths [Advance Release],* 60.2

price spike has subsided somewhat since then, overall REO prices/kg in 2013 remain well above year-end 2010 levels.

Taken in the context of China's *de facto* monopoly on global REE output, this combination of sharply higher prices and steeply reduced supply sets the stage for new state actors to enter the REO marketplace to sate the increasing global demand for these strategic resources. Vietnam stands poised to become a key player in these future supplies.

### Vietnamese REO Deposits

Rare earth oxide deposits were discovered in Vietnam as early as 1958, including two large ore bodies in the northwest province of Lai Chau, as well as mineral sands of lesser value in some coastal areas. Geological surveys and evaluation were carried out in 1958-1969 at the two ore body sites, known as Nam Xe and Dong Pao. As REOs were only of limited economic value at the time of these finds, Vietnam took no measures to develop the deposits, and prior to 1990 had extracted only 100 tons of REOs in a cooperative venture with Poland, Czechoslovakia and East Germany, primarily for assay and experimentation purposes.[18] In the years since then, three additional major deposits of REOs have been located: at Muong Hum in Lao Cai province, at Yen Phu in Yen Bai province, and at Then Chau in Lai Chau province (see Figure 4). While full assay reports are unavailable for these latter three finds, what data is available indicates that these five ore

**Figure 4.** Location of Vietnamese REO ore bodies. **Source:** Graphic created by author. Vietnam map from www.d-maps.com.

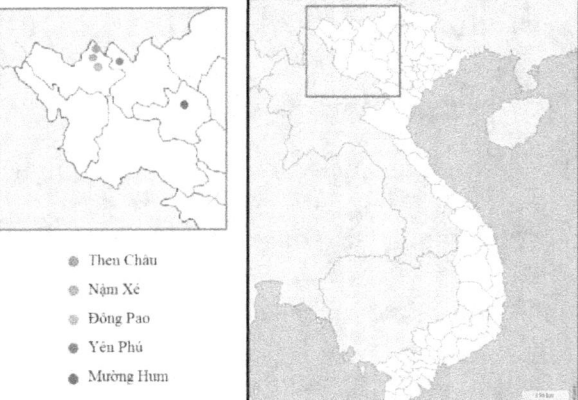

- Then Châu
- Nậm Xé
- Đông Pao
- Yên Phú
- Mường Hum

---

[18] United Nations Economic and Social Commission for Asia and the Pacific. *Atlas of Mineral Resources of the ESCAP Region, Vol. 6, Viet Nam*, 101.

bodies contain proven and probable reserves of a minimum of 11 million tons of REOs, broken down as follows: Nam Xe – 7.7 million tons; Dong Pao – 3.17 million tons; Muong Hum – 400,000 tons; Yen Phu – 5,000 tons; and Then Chau – 194,000 tons.[19] Sampling and evaluation studies have further shown that the deposits at Nam Xe have a possible 10 million tons of REO ore reserves beyond the figure already cited.[20] These numbers compare favorably with those of China (estimated 36 million tons of reserves) and the United States (13 million tons), and place Vietnam solidly among the top tier of countries with significant REO reserves.[21]

Among the Vietnamese deposits, those at Nam Xe and Dong Pao are notable for their vast size. The larger of the two, Nam Xe, is even more significant due to its mineral content. Assays of the Nam Xe ore bodies indicate that this deposit is exceptionally rich in the higher-value HREEs, especially including yttrium, europium, and gadolinium (see Figure 5).[22] As has already been noted, deposits with relatively high concentrations of HREEs, yttrium, and europium are far scarcer than those

**Figure 5.** Composition of Nam Xe REO ores as compared to Chinese and U.S. deposits.
**Source:** http://pubs.usgs.gov/fs/2002/fs087-02/fs087-02.pdf, modified by the author to include data on Vietnam.

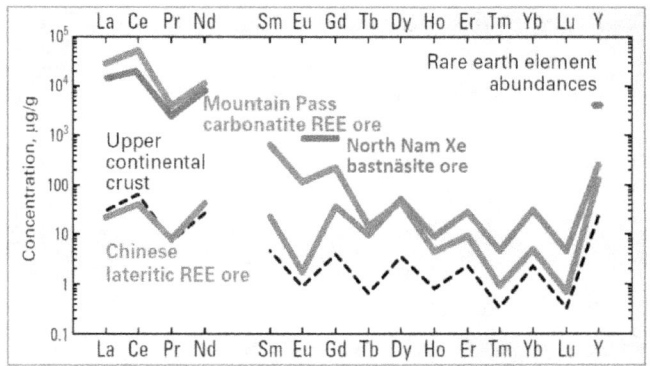

[19] Data compiled from: United Nations Economic and Social Commission for Asia and the Pacific. *Atlas of Mineral Resources of the ESCAP Region, Vol. 6, Viet Nam*, 101-103; Nakamura, Shigeo. "Current Trends of Rare Earth Market in Japan." PowerPoint presentation, Critical Metals Investment Symposium, Vancouver, Canada, January 21, 2011; Than, Van Lien and Truong Giang Nguyen. "The Assessment of Thorium Resources in Vietnam." PowerPoint presentation, IAEA Technical Meeting on Thorium Resources and Provinces, Vienna, Austria, September 24, 2013; U.S. Department of the Interior, U.S. Geological Survey. *2011 Minerals Yearbook: Vietnam [Advance Release]*, 28.6.
[20] United Nations Economic and Social Commission for Asia and the Pacific. *Atlas of Mineral Resources of the ESCAP Region, Vol. 6, Viet Nam*, 102.
[21] "2011 Spells Desperate Search for Rare Earth Minerals." *International Business Times*, January 8, 2011.
[22] United Nations Economic and Social Commission for Asia and the Pacific. *Atlas of Mineral Resources of the ESCAP Region, Vol. 6, Viet Nam*, 102-3.

containing more-commonly found LREEs. The unusual abundance of these HREEs among the ore bodies at Nam Xe make REO mining activity at that location a highly profitable prospect. At present however, Vietnam has only one operating mine producing REO ore, recently brought on-line at Dong Pao. Annual production in 2013 from ore mined at that location is estimated to reach just 3,000 tons of REEs.[23] Clearly there is far greater potential in Vietnam for REO extraction and REE production, but until recently, development was slowed by heavy restrictions on foreign mining activity; it is likely that general international uncertainty about the long-term viability of investment in Vietnam played a role as well. With the coming into effect of the *2010 Mineral Law* on July 1, 2011, some of these restrictions and concerns have been alleviated. However, the Mineral Law requires national 30-year implementation strategies be adopted for each class of minerals, and specifies that until those strategies have been drafted and approved, new mining activity is to be limited. Reinforcing this concept, in December 2011 the government of Vietnam took an interim decision that prior to development of the 30-year implementation strategy for REOs, "[all] mining, processing and export of rare earth elements…are subject to approval of the Prime Minister."[24] This clearly signals that Vietnam has recognized the importance of their REO ore bodies; what remains is for Vietnam to adopt a comprehensive path forward on the beneficial exploitation of these valuable resources.

### Outside Interest in Vietnamese REOs/REEs

The value of Vietnam's REO deposits as an alternative to reliance on Chinese supplies has not gone unnoticed by the outside world. Indeed, in the wake of China's 2010

---

[23] Hur, Jae and Ichiro Suzuki. "Japan to Secure 20% of Rare-Earth Requirements From Vietnam." *Bloomberg.com*, October 28, 2011.
[24] The Prime Minister of the Socialist Republic of Vietnam, *Directive No. 02/CT-TTg of January 9, 2012, on Strengthening State Management of Exploration, Exploitation, Processing, Use and Export of Minerals.*

temporary embargo of REO exports to Japan, two regional state actors – Japan and Singapore – have stepped forward to aggressively pursue REO development, mining and processing rights in Vietnam.

Japan was the first state actor to approach Vietnam as a potential supply of REEs, doing so in the very midst of the Chinese embargo. On October 22, 2010 – just one month into the embargo – Japan's Trade Ministry announced that Toyota Tsusho would commence work together with Sojitz Corporation in Vietnam to mine REOs. A Trade Ministry representative underlined broad Government of Japan support for the move, stating that "[it] is too risky to depend on one country for crucial material supplies."[25] Progress on the announced project has been swift. By February 2011, Toyota Tsusho had clarified its investment plans, specifying its intent to invest $130 million in Lai Chau province (specifically at Dong Pao) for rare earth production.[26] Further impetus was given to the cooperative venture on October 31, 2011, during Vietnamese Prime Minister Tan Dung Nguyen's state visit to Japan, when he signed a formal agreement with Japanese Prime Minister Yoshihiko Noda to promote "cooperation in the investigation, exploration, exploitation and processing of rare earths in Vietnam."[27]

Following the completion of this formal agreement, the government of Japan, working through the Japan Oil, Gas and Metals National Corporation (JOGMEC), provided $5.3 million of equipment towards opening of a rare earth research center in Hanoi in June 2012, with a stated goal for the center of researching production of finished rare earth

---

[25] Yuasa, Shino. "Rare Earth Metals Will be Mined in Vietnam by the Japanese." *The Christian Science Monitor*, October 22, 2010.

[26] Hur, Jae and Ichiro Suzuki. "Japan to Secure 20% of Rare-Earth Requirements From Vietnam." *Bloomberg.com*, October 28, 2011.

[27] The Prime Minister of Japan and His Cabinet. "Japan-Viet Nam Joint Statement on the Actions Taken Under Strategic Partnership for Peace and Prosperity in Asia." October 31, 2011.

products.[28] This center is the first facility in Vietnam capable of separating REEs from REO ores.

On October 8, 2012, the Vietnam National Coal and Mineral Industries Group (VINACOMIN) inked a formal agreement to begin mining activity for the REOs Japan seeks in 2013, with planned production of raw ore set to reach 720,000 tons/year by 2015. To put this into perspective, the figure of 3.17 million tons of REO reserves noted earlier for the Dong Pao deposit was calculated from an average REO content of 3.0-10.7% per ton of raw ore; extrapolated, this would yield a lifetime of between 37 and 147 years for the Dong Pao mine at the planned level of activity. The research and production center mentioned above will process the ores into export-quality refined REEs and REE products, with production of these estimated at 3,000 tons in 2013, rising to 7,000 tons in 2014.[29] These production numbers should reach up to 10,000 tons/year once full capacity is reached in the near future.[30] Even at 2014 production levels, the REEs produced from this venture alone will supply 20% of Japan's annual REE requirements, a significant step towards security against future Chinese export restrictions.[31]

In a similar move, on December 5, 2012, the Singaporean firm Winglee Resources PTE announced its investment of $17.4 million for a 49% stake in a new rare earth processing and manufacturing plant in Ha Long, Vietnam. Due to come on-line by the end of 2013, this facility – which will be the second such in Vietnam, following the Japanese

---

[28] Fuyuno, Ichiko. "Japan and Vietnam Join Forces to Exploit Rare Earths." *Nature*, July 13, 2012.
[29] Hur, Jae and Ichiro Suzuki. "Japan to Secure 20% of Rare-Earth Requirements From Vietnam." *Bloomberg.com*, October 28, 2011.
[30] "VINACOMIN and Japanese Firm to Exploit and Process Rare Earth in Lai Chau." *Vietnam National Coal-Mineral Industries Holding Corporation Limited (VINACOMIN)*, August 10, 2012.
[31] Hur, Jae and Ichiro Suzuki. "Japan to Secure 20% of Rare-Earth Requirements From Vietnam." *Bloomberg.com*, October 28, 2011.

facility in Hanoi – has a planned production of 3,000 tons/year of refined REEs and REE products once full capacity is reached.[32]

These two large ventures, undertaken by firms based in countries that are entirely reliant on Chinese REO/REE supply sources, illustrate the seriousness with which public and private enterprises in Asia are taking China's export restrictions of the past several years. It is also significant that both undertakings involve production and processing within Vietnam of native REO ores into much more valuable concentrated REO powders or final REE products for export. This is no accident; pursuant to Vietnam's *2010 Mining Law*, clarifying directions issued by the Prime Minister have indicated that as a general principle, "mining of minerals must be associated with processing, creating products of high economic value."[33] Implementing regulations issued by the Ministry of Industry and Trade have specified that export of REOs is restricted to REO powders ≥99% purity, with no allowance for the export of raw ore.[34]

### Illegal Mining and Associated Risks

The Ministry's regulations notwithstanding, Vietnam already has a burgeoning trade in raw REO ores. The proximity of the Vietnamese REO ore bodies to the Chinese border has stimulated an illegal export trade in raw REO-laden bastnäsite ore. Reportedly, local residents near Dong Pao run 200-kg loads of bastnäsite to ore traders who then move it across the border into China, earning an average $50 per load.[35] During 2012 alone, Lai

---

[32] "US$ 35.5 Million High-Tech Rare Earth Processing Plant to be Built in Quang Ninh." *Quang Ninh Portal*, December 5, 2012.

[33] The Prime Minister of the Socialist Republic of Vietnam, *Decision No. 2427/QD-TTg of the Prime Minister dated December 22, 2011 on Approval of the Mineral Strategy to 2020, with Vision to 2030 (Decision 2427)*, Article 1(3)(c).

[34] The Ministry of Industry and Trade of the Socialist Republic of Vietnam, *Circular No. 41/2012/TT-BCT of the Ministry of Industry and Trade of December 21, 2012, on Providing the Export of Minerals*, Appendix §7.

[35] Son, Na. "Lai Chau: Locals Steal Rare Earth Ore." *Look at Vietnam*, June 11, 2012.

Chau officials closed down eleven illegal mining operations in the vicinity.[36]  While this sort of freelance-capitalist enterprise does highlight the importance of Vietnam as a source for REOs, the Vietnamese government will have to seek to quash such illegal activity, lest it undermine foreign firms' confidence in the value of their investments.  This illegal mining activity is also dangerous to those involved; as already noted, bastnäsite is generally rich in NORMs (including uranium and thorium) as well as REOs.  Studies have shown that at the Dong Pao deposits, without appropriate protection measures, illegal miners risk personal exposure to direct gamma radiation of up to 40 mSv/year, as well as exposure to Radon gas in concentrations as high as hundreds of $Bq/m^3$ of air; the recommended safety limits for civilian exposure are 3.5 mSv/year and 0.15 $Bq/m^3$, respectively.[37]

### REO Mining – a Potential Source for Uranium

Although the radioactive nature of the Vietnam REO deposits requires special handling to exploit them safely, far from being a liability, Vietnam should welcome the NORMs associated with these ore bodies as a source for another much-needed strategic mineral: uranium.

The five REO ore bodies in Vietnam contain estimated proven and probable reserves of approximately 80,000 tons of uranium, primarily in the form of triuranium octoxide ($U_3O_8$), distributed as follows:  Nam Xe – 76,000 tons; Dong Pao – 1900 tons; Muong Hum – 1000 tons; and Then Chau – 1000 tons.[38]  Based on October 2013 prices for $U_3O_8$, this

---

[36] "Lai Chau Tightens Controls on Mining." *Vietnam Breaking News*, March 13, 2013.

[37] Nguyen, Van Nam, Thai Son Nguyen and Quang Vinh Nguyen. "Study on the Characteristics of Natural Radioactive Fields for the Assessment of Radioactive Pollution on Rare Earth Deposits in Northern Vietnam." PowerPoint presentation, General Department of Geology and Minerals of Vietnam, undated.

[38] Data from two sources: United Nations Economic and Social Commission for Asia and the Pacific. *Atlas of Mineral Resources of the ESCAP Region, Vol. 6, Viet Nam*, 102-104; Than, Van Lien and Truong Giang Nguyen. "The Assessment of Thorium Resources in Vietnam." PowerPoint presentation, IAEA Technical Meeting on Thorium Resources and Provinces, Vienna, Austria, September 24, 2013.

represents \$6.2 billion worth of ore.[39]  While this does represent a significant quantity of $U_3O_8$, none of the five REO ore bodies in Vietnam contain what mining firms would consider a high concentration of uranium ore (>0.1%).  The richest deposit is Dong Pao, where triuranium octoxide is found in concentrations ranging across the ore body of 0.04-0.08%.[40]  These relatively low concentrations of $U_3O_8$ would normally rule out exploiting the five REO deposits for uranium alone.  However, as Vietnam is already getting into the business of processing ore from these sites to extract the REEs, it would be only logical to set up an ancillary operation to process the tailings from this first step to provide a domestic supply of uranium, perhaps obviating the need to open separate mines specifically for that element.  In Kazakhstan a Japanese joint venture is already planning such an operation – though to do the opposite: extracting REOs from the tailings of the now-defunct uranium mine at the western city of Aktau – due to the lower costs of reprocessing previously-mined ore compared to undertaking new mining activity.[41]  Triuranium octoxide is the most stable of the uranium oxides, and is the primary component of yellowcake – an intermediate step in processing uranium ores into low-enriched uranium (LEU) fuel.[42]  Vietnam's Mineral Strategy to 2020 with Vision to 2030 encourages exactly this sort of activity as a key goal – in order to provide the "raw materials for nuclear power plants."[43]

---

[39] *Trade Tech: Uranium Prices & Analysis,* http://www.uranium.info/in_the_market.php, October 25, 2013.

[40] United Nations Economic and Social Commission for Asia and the Pacific. *Atlas of Mineral Resources of the ESCAP Region, Vol. 6, Viet Nam*, 101-103.

[41] Orininskaya, Olga and Robin Paxton. "Kazakhs Launch Rare Earths-from-Uranium-Tailings Project with Sumitomo." *Mineweb*, March 25, 2011.

[42] U.S. Nuclear Regulatory Commission. "Yellowcake Fact Sheet."

[43] The Prime Minister of the Socialist Republic of Vietnam, *Decision No. 2427/QD-TTg of the Prime Minister dated December 22, 2011 on Approval of the Mineral Strategy to 2020, with Vision to 2030 (Decision 2427)*, Article 1(4)(b).

## Vietnam's Nuclear Dreams

At present Vietnam has only one 500 MW research reactor at Da Lat, which was originally brought online by General Electric in 1963, and heavily rebuilt by Soviet engineers in the early 1980s.[44] Nonetheless, Vietnam's ambitious plan to establish a domestic nuclear power-generating capability calls for constructing 13 nuclear reactors, in order to provide 10.1% of total domestic power generation by 2030.[45] The first tranche includes a two-reactor, $10.6 billion plant capable of generating 2.4 GW, to be constructed in collaboration with the Russian company Atomstroyexport beginning in 2014, with completion projected for 2020. A second, $14.4 billion, two-reactor plant set to generate 2 GW, will be built between 2014-2022 by the International Nuclear Energy Development Corporation of Japan.[46] In March 2012, South Korea was named as the preferred bidder for an additional $20 billion plant.[47]

Obviously, all of these plants will need fuel. Vietnam, however, does not have the domestic capacity to produce LEU fuel – and has just signed an agreement that forbids developing such a capability. On the margins of the October 10, 2013 ASEAN summit in Brunei, Vietnamese Foreign Minister Pham Binh Minh and U.S. Secretary of State John Kerry concluded an agreement that reportedly "prohibits Vietnam from enriching or

---

[44] Nguyen, Kien Cuong. "The Role of a Research Reactor in the National Nuclear Energy Programme in Vietnam: Present and Future." PowerPoint presentation, IAEA International Conference on Research Reactors, Rabat, Morocco, November 14, 2011.
[45] The Prime Minister of the Socialist Republic of Vietnam, *Decision No. 1208/QD-TTg of July 21, 2011 on Approval of the National Master Plan for Power Development for the 2011-2020 Period with Vision to 2030 (Master Power Plan VII),* Article 1(3)(a).
[46] Business Monitor International. *Vietnam Power Report Q4 2013*, 37.
[47] "Natural Resources, Vietnam." *Jane's Sentinel Security Assessment- Southeast Asia*, July 5, 2012, 6.

processing plutonium or uranium while developing nuclear energy."[48] So how will Vietnam fuel these atomic fires?

### U.S. Interests: Diversity of REE Supplies and Provision of Uranium Fuel

Though the text is not yet publicly available, the Peaceful Uses of Nuclear Energy Agreement initialed in Brunei reportedly includes a statement of U.S. interest in selling LEU fuel to Vietnam, and, according to one U.S. official, "the agreement provides the basis for U.S. firms to enter the market early as it builds nuclear power plants and for the U.S. government to ensure the proper safeguards."[49] Promoting U.S. firms that bid on construction of Vietnam's remaining nine planned reactors and encouraging sales of U.S.-produced LEU fuel are both potentially lucrative endeavors. At the signing ceremony, Secretary Kerry noted that "Vietnam has the second-largest market, after China, for nuclear power in East Asia, and our companies can now compete. What is a $10 billion market today is expected to grow into a $50 billion market by the year 2030."[50]

Increasing U.S. exports is a key part of President Obama's trade policies. In this particular instance, there is still another opportunity: given the potential for reprocessing REO ore tailings to extract $U_3O_8$ as a step towards producing LEU fuel, there is a natural linkage between Vietnam's LEU fuel needs and the United States' need to diversify its REE supply chain.

The House Committee on Armed Services has reported that "each SSN-774 *Virginia*-class submarine would require approximately 9,200 pounds of rare earth materials, each DDG-51 Aegis destroyer would require approximately 5,200 pounds of these materials, and

---

[48] Lakhshmanan, Indira A.R. and David Lerman. "U.S. Reaches Deal to Provide Vietnam Civilian Nuclear Power." *Bloomberg.com*, October 10, 2013.
[49] Wroughton, Lesley. "US, Vietnam Sign Nuclear Trade Agreement." *Reuters*, October 10, 2013.
[50] "Agreement opens US-Vietnam nuclear trade." *World Nuclear News,* October 10, 2013.

each F-35 Lightning II aircraft would require approximately 920 pounds of these materials."[51] The critical importance of REEs in these key national defense systems led Congress in 2010 to request detailed information on Department of Defense (DOD) access to supplies of REEs. The request required DOD to report on REEs which were both "critical to the production, sustainment, or operation of significant United States military equipment" and "subject to interruption of supply, based on actions or events outside the control of the government of the United States."[52] In response, an interim DOD report from 2012 surveyed the state of U.S. REE supplies, and found that seven REEs were reportable under these criteria: dysprosium, erbium, europium, gadolinium, neodymium, praseodymium, and yttrium. The report optimistically suggested, however, that "by 2013 U.S. production could satisfy the level of consumption required to meet defense procurement needs, with the exception of yttrium."[53] Following further Congressional inquiry on the matter, DOD again reviewed the state of U.S. REE supplies in 2013, and this time found critical shortages of six REEs: dysprosium, erbium, terbium, thulium, scandium, and yttrium; clearly the optimism of the earlier report was unfounded. The recommendation of this latter report was that the United States should commence stockpiling $130 million worth of HREEs immediately, most particularly yttrium.[54] As these Congressional inquiries have brought to light, continued U.S. dependence on China as a sole supplier for these strategic minerals is distinctly a critical vulnerability.

---

[51] U.S. Congress. House of Representatives. *National Defense Authorization Act for Fiscal year 2014: Report of the Committee on Armed Services, House of Representatives on H.R. 1960.* 113th Cong., 1st sess., June 7, 2013.
[52] *Ike Skelton National Defense Authorization Act for Fiscal Year 2011*, Public Law 111-383, U.S. Statutes at Large 124 (2010): 4137, § 843.
[53] U.S. Department of Defense, Office of the Undersecretary of Defense for Acquisition, Technology and Logistics. *Report to Congress: Rare Earth Materials in Defense Applications*. March 2012.
[54] U.S. Department of Defense, Office of the Undersecretary of Defense for Acquisition, Technology and Logistics. *Strategic and Critical Materials 2013 Report on Stockpile Requirements*. January 2013, 5.

The common thread in the two DOD reports is the highlighting of yttrium as the REE of most vital concern. Fortuitously, the Vietnamese REO ore bodies are significantly rich in yttrium – a fact which makes Vietnam an attractive partner in the search for diversity of REE supplies. Coupled with the possibility of promoting U.S. sales of LEU fuel made from reprocessing previously-mined REO ores, Vietnam looks even more attractive.

## Conclusion

The information presented in the preceding discussion highlights some of the potential courses of action which states wishing to cooperate with Vietnam in developing its untapped rare earth mineral resources could take. It is clear that Vietnam is committed to REO mining, and its cooperative ventures with foreign partners – particularly with Japan – demonstrate the significant opportunity for foreign state actors to reduce their dependence on Chinese rare earth supplies through investment in Vietnam's developing rare earth mining sector. In the same way, Vietnam's robust plan for growing a domestic nuclear-power program through technical cooperation with Japan, South Korea, Russia and the United States presents an important opening for foreign firms to engage in sales of nuclear-power technology and uranium fuel.

Both of these commercial opportunities point towards a nexus of U.S. strategic interests: promoting safe, secure and peaceful nuclear technologies vis-à-vis Vietnam's nuclear ambitions as well as promoting sales of American technology and LEU fuel; and the possibility of reducing dependence on China as the sole source for REEs essential to our national defense supply chain. It is to be hoped that the United States does not let this opportunity pass by.

## Recommendations

- The United States should aggressively pursue a policy seeking to obtain refined REEs critical to national defense from the Republic of Vietnam, as an alternative to Chinese supply sources, and as part of an overall pattern of seeking to diversify REE suppliers.

- In conjunction with the above, the United States should expand upon the agreement reached at the 2013 ASEAN summit with Vietnam on sales of LEU fuel, by seeking to provide these fuels from enrichment of the $U_3O_8$ to be obtained through reprocessing ore supplied from REO mining activities in Vietnam.

## Selected Bibliography

"2011 Spells Desperate Search for Rare Earth Minerals." *International Business Times*, January 8, 2011. http://www.ibtimes.com/2011-spells-desperate-search-rare-earth-minerals-253177 (accessed October 17, 2013).

"Agreement opens US-Vietnam nuclear trade." *World Nuclear News,* October 10, 2013. http://www.world-nuclear-news.org/NP-Agreement_opens_US_Vietnam_nuclear_trade-1010134.html (accessed October 27, 2013).

Areddy, James T. and Chuin-Wei Yap. "China Raises Rare-Earth Export Quota." *The Wall Street Journal*, August 22, 2012. http://online.wsj.com/news/articles/SB10000872396390443989204577604324226426682 (accessed October 27, 2013).

Business Monitor International. *Vietnam Power Report Q4 2013.* London, United Kingdom: Business Monitor International, 2013.

Butts, Kent Hughes, Brent Bankus, and Adam Norris. "Strategic Minerals – Is China's Consumption a Threat to United States Security?" *U.S. Army War College Center for Strategic Leadership Issue Paper*, Volume 7-11 (July 2011). http://www.csl.army.mil/usacsl/publications/IP7_11.pdf (accessed September 15, 2013).

Congsan, Dang. "Hausse des exportations de minerai et de minéraux." [Increase in Exports of Ore and Minerals.] *ParlerVietnam.com,* August 23, 2013. http://parlervietnam.com/2013/08/hausse-des-exportations-de-minerai-et-de-mineraux/#.Uj4Zhj_ZyuA (accessed September 21, 2013).

"Fuelling the Demand – Nuclear Power in Asia." *Jane's Intelligence Review*, October 16, 2012. https://www.janes.ihs.com/CustomPages/Janes/Home.aspx (accessed September 8, 2013).

Fuyuno, Ichiko. "Japan and Vietnam Join Forces to Exploit Rare Earths." *Nature*, July 13, 2012. http://www.nature.com/news/japan-and-vietnam-join-forces-to-exploit-rare-earth-elements-1.11009 (accessed October 5, 2013).

"Geography, Vietnam." *Jane's Sentinel Security Assessment- Southeast Asia*, June 15, 2012. https://www.janes.ihs.com/CustomPages/Janes/Home.aspx (accessed September 8, 2013).

*Горная энциклопедия* [Encyclopedia of Mining], online edition, *s.v.* "Vietnam." http://www.mining-enc.ru/v/vetnam/ (accessed September 8, 2013).

Hawkins, Kevin, and Orsolya Szotyory-Grove. "Vietnam's Long-Term Strategy for Exploitation of Mineral Resources." *Mayer Brown JSM Legal Update*, June 1, 2012. http://www.mayerbrown.com/Vietnams-Long-Term-Strategy-for-Exploitation-of-Mineral-Resources-06-01-2012 (accessed September 6, 2013).

Hur, Jae and Ichiro Suzuki. "Japan to Secure 20% of Rare-Earth Requirements From Vietnam." *Bloomberg.com*, October 28, 2011. http://www.bloomberg.com/news/2011-10-28/japan-to-secure-20-of-rare-earth-requirements-from-vietnam.html (accessed October 5, 2013).

*Ike Skelton National Defense Authorization Act for Fiscal Year 2011*, Public Law 111-383, U.S. Statutes at Large 124 (2010): 4137.

Kosich, Dorothy. "China Announces Second REE Quota for 2013." *Mineweb*, July 2, 2013. http://www.mineweb.com/mineweb/content/en/mineweb-industrial-metals-minerals-old?oid=196267&sn=Detail (accessed October 27, 2013).

Orininskaya, Olga and Robin Paxton. "Kazakhs Launch Rare Earths-from-Uranium-Tailings Project with Sumitomo." *Mineweb*, March 25, 2011. http://www.mineweb.com/mineweb/content/en/mineweb-uranium?oid=123670&sn=Detail (accessed October 27, 2013).

"Lai Chau Tightens Controls on Mining." *Vietnam Breaking News*, March 13, 2013. http://vietnambreakingnews.com/2013/03/lai-chau-tightens-controls-on-mining/#.UmFjahCFf3B (accessed October 17, 2013).

Lakhshmanan, Indira A.R. and David Lerman. "U.S. Reaches Deal to Provide Vietnam Civilian Nuclear Power." *Bloomberg.com*, October 10, 2013. http://www.bloomberg.com/news/2013-10-10/u-s-reaches-deal-to-provide-civilian-nuclear-power-to-vietnam.html (accessed October 14, 2013).

Le, Doan Phac. "Programme for Nuclear Power Development in Vietnam." PowerPoint Presentation, IAEA/INPRO Consultants' Meeting on Survey of Existing National Long Range Nuclear Energy Strategies, Vienna, Austria, March 23, 2012.

"Lots of Opportunities for Vietnam's Mining Industries." *Vietnam National Coal-Mineral Industries Holding Corporation Limited (VINACOMIN)*, December 25, 2012. http://www.vinacomin.vn/en/news/News-and-Mining/Lots-of-Opportunities-for-Vietnam-s-Mining-Industry-426.html (accessed September 22, 2013).

Ly, Huong. "Vietnam Mining Industry: Significant Room for Growth." Vietnam Chamber of Commerce and Industry. http://www.vccinews.com/news_detail.asp?news_id=22489 (accessed September 21, 2013).

Meisels, A. Greer. "The Rare Earth Race." *The National Interest*, June 26, 2012. http://nationalinterest.org/commentary/the-race-rare-earth-elements-7120 (accessed September 22, 2013).

Nakamura, Shigeo. "Current Trends of Rare Earth Market in Japan." PowerPoint presentation, Critical Metals Investment Symposium, Vancouver, Canada, January 21, 2011.

"Natural Resources, Vietnam." *Jane's Sentinel Security Assessment- Southeast Asia*, July 5, 2012. https://www.janes.ihs.com/CustomPages/Janes/Home.aspx (accessed September 8, 2013).

Nguyen, Dao and Kevin Hawkins. "Vietnam Power Development Plan for the 2011-2020 Period." *Mayer Brown JSM Legal Update*, September 1, 2011. http://www.mayerbrown.com/publications/Vietnam-Power-Development-Plan-for-the-2011-2020-Period-09-01-2011 (accessed October 2, 2013).

Nguyen, Dao, Toby Nicholas Rees, Hong Ha Nguyen, and Thinh Dahn. "Vietnam's 2010 Mineral Law." *Mayer Brown JSM Legal Update*, March 14, 2011. http://www.mayerbrown.com/publications/Vietnams-2010-Mineral-Law-03-14-2011 (accessed September 21, 2013).

Nguyen, Kien Cuong. "The Role of a Research Reactor in the National Nuclear Energy Programme in Vietnam: Present and Future." PowerPoint presentation, IAEA International Conference on Research Reactors, Rabat, Morocco, November 14, 2011.

Nguyen, Van Nam, Thai Son Nguyen and Quang Vinh Nguyen. "Study on the Characteristics of Natural Radioactive Fields for the Assessment of Radioactive Pollution on Rare Earth Deposits in Northern Vietnam." PowerPoint presentation, General Department of Geology and Minerals of Vietnam, undated. http://www.dgmv.gov.vn/index.php?option=com_k2&view=item&id=5809:study-on-the-characteristics-of-natural-radioactive-fields-for-the-assessment-of-radioactive-pollution-on-rave-earth-deposits-in-northern-vietnam&Itemid=379&lang=en (accessed October 12, 2013).

"Obama Announces WTO Case Against China over Rare Earths." *CNN*, March 13, 2012. http://www.cnn.com/2012/03/13/world/asia/china-rare-earths-case (accessed September 27, 2013).

Onishi, Norimitsu. "Vietnam's Nuclear Dreams Blossom Despite Doubts." *New York Times,* March 1, 2012. http://www.nytimes.com/2012/03/02/world/asia/vietnams-nuclear-dreams-blossom-despite-doubts.html?pagewanted=all&_r=0 (accessed September 12, 2013).

Pillai, P.M.B., "Naturally Occurring Radioactive Material (NORM) in the Extraction and Processing of Rare Earths," in *Naturally Occurring Radioactive Material (NORM V): Proceedings of the Fifth International Symposium on Naturally Occurring Radioactive Material Organized by the University of Seville, et al., held in Seville, 19-22 March 2007,* ed. International Atomic Energy Agency. Vienna, Austria: International Atomic Energy Agency, 2008.

Rowley, Emma. "Rare Earths: West Bids to Challenge China's Monopoly, but is it Too Late?" *The Telegraph* (London), August 19, 2013. http://www.telegraph.co.uk/finance/commodities/10253189/Rare-earths-West-bids-to-challenge-Chinas-monopoly-but-is-it-too-late.html (accessed September 6, 2013).

"Russia, Vietnam to Advance High-Tech Co-operation." *Jane's Defence Industry*, March 17, 2010. https://www.janes.ihs.com/CustomPages/Janes/Home.aspx (accessed September 8, 2013).

Sokolski, Henry. "Obama's Nuclear Vietnam." *National Review,* June 4, 2013. http://www.nationalreview.com/energy-week/350043/obamas-nuclear-vietnam-henry-sokolski (accessed September 12, 2013).

Son, Na. "Lai Chau: Locals Steal Rare Earth Ore." *Look at Vietnam*, June 11, 2012. http://www.lookatvietnam.com/2012/06/lai-chau-locals-steal-rare-earth-ore.html (accessed October 17, 2013).

Thai, Tran. "Rare, Not Scarce." *Ministry of Natural Resources and Environment of Vietnam*, February 15, 2011. http://www.monre.gov.vn/v35/default.aspx?tabid =675&CateID=57&ID=96176&Code=YT09996176 (accessed October 14, 2013).

Than, Van Lien and Truong Giang Nguyen. "The Assessment of Thorium Resources in Vietnam." PowerPoint presentation, IAEA Technical Meeting on Thorium Resources and Provinces, Vienna, Austria, September 24, 2013.

Thayer, Carlyle A. "The Russia-Vietnam Comprehensive Partnership." *East Asia Forum* (Canberra), October 9, 2012. http://www.eastasiaforum.org/2012/10/09/the-russia-vietnam-comprehensive-partnership (accessed September 6, 2013).

The Ministry of Industry and Trade of the Socialist Republic of Vietnam. *Circular No. 41/2012/TT-BCT of the Ministry of Industry and Trade dated December 21, 2012, on Providing the Export of Minerals.* December 21, 2012. http://www.customs.gov.vn/ Lists/EnglishDocuments/Attachments/1142/Circular%20No.41%2712%20BCT.doc (accessed October 22, 2013).

The National Assembly of the Socialist Republic of Vietnam. *Law No. 60/2010/QH12 of November 17, 2010 on Mineral Law (2010 Mineral Law).* November 17, 2010. http://www.epronews.com/en-US/Document/Details.aspx?ID=282 (accessed October 6, 2013).

The Prime Minister of Japan and His Cabinet. "Japan-Viet Nam Joint Statement on the Actions Taken Under Strategic Partnership for Peace and Prosperity in Asia." October 31, 2011. http://www.kantei.go.jp/foreign/noda/diplomatic/201110/ 31vietnam_e.html (accessed October 12, 2013).

The Prime Minister of the Socialist Republic of Vietnam. *Decision No. 1208/QD-TTg of July 21, 2011 on Approval of the National Master Plan for Power Development for the 2011-2020 Period with the Vision to 2030 (Power Master Plan VII).* July 21, 2011. http://www.nti.org/media/pdfs/VietnamPowerDevelopmentPlan2030.pdf?_=1333146 022 (accessed October 2, 2013).

The Prime Minister of the Socialist Republic of Vietnam. *Decision No. 2427/QD-TTg of the Prime Minister dated December 22, 2011 on Approval of the Mineral Strategy to 2020, with Vision to 2030 (Decision 2427).* December 22, 2011. http://vbqppl.mpi.

gov.vn/en-us/Pages/default.aspx?itemId=43f92b01-8a30-414b-bb90-8c475dad497e&list=documentDetail (accessed October 22, 2013).

The Prime Minister of the Socialist Republic of Vietnam. *Directive No. 02/CT-TTg of January 9, 2012, on Strengthening State Management of Exploration, Exploitation, Processing, Use and Export of Minerals.* January 9, 2012. http://vbqppl.mpi.gov.vn/en-us/Pages/default.aspx?itemId=b5fd3f24-63ed-4a40-8ae9-631c70bea7e6&list=documentDetail (accessed October 22, 2013).

Tse, Pui-Kwan. *China's Rare-Earth Industry: U.S. Geological Survey Open-File Report 2011–1042.* (Washington, DC: Department of the Interior, 2011).

United Nations Economic and Social Commission for Asia and the Pacific. *Atlas of Mineral Resources of the ESCAP Region, Vol. 6, Viet Nam.* ST/ESCAP/831. Bangkok: UNESCAP, 1990.

"US$ 35.5 Million High-Tech Rare Earth Processing Plant to be Built in Quang Ninh." *Quang Ninh Portal*, December 5, 2012. http://www.quangninh.gov.vn/en-us/Pages/Tin%20chi%20ti%E1%BA%BFt.aspx?newsid=745&dt=2012-12-05&cid=1 (accessed October 5, 2013).

U.S. Congress. House of Representatives. *National Defense Authorization Act for Fiscal year 2014: Report of the Committee on Armed Services, House of Representatives on H.R. 1960.* 113th Cong., 1st sess., June 7, 2013. http://www.gpo.gov/fdsys/pkg/CRPT-113hrpt102/pdf/CRPT-113hrpt102.pdf (accessed October 13, 2013).

U.S. Department of Defense, Office of the Undersecretary of Defense for Acquisition, Technology and Logistics. *Report to Congress: Rare Earth Materials in Defense Applications.* March 2012. http://www.hsdl.org/?view&did=704803 (accessed September 20, 2013.

U.S. Department of Defense, Office of the Undersecretary of Defense for Acquisition, Technology and Logistics. *Strategic and Critical Materials 2013 Report on Stockpile Requirements.* January 2013. http://mineralsmakelife.org/assets/images/content/resources/Strategic%20and%20Critical%20Materials%202013%20Report%20on%20Stockpile%20Requirements.pdf (accessed October 19, 2013).

U.S. Department of the Interior, U.S. Geological Survey. *2011 Minerals Yearbook: Rare Earths [Advance Release].* (Washington, DC: Department of the Interior, September, 2013).

—. *2011 Minerals Yearbook: Vietnam [Advance Release].* (Washington, DC: Department of the Interior, July, 2013).

—. *Mineral Commodity Summaries 2013.* (Washington, DC: Department of the Interior, January, 2013).

—. *U.S, Geological Survey Fact Sheet 087-02: Rare Earth Elements – Critical Resources for High Technology.* (Washington, DC: Department of the Interior, 2002).

U.S. Environmental Protection Agency, *Rare Earth Elements: A Review of Production, Processing, Recycling, and Associated Environmental Issues*. EPA/600/R-12/572. Washington, DC: Environmental Protection Agency, 2012.

U.S. Library of Congress, Congressional Research Service. *Rare Earth Elements: The Global Supply Chain*, by Marc Humphries. CRS Report R41347. Washington, DC: Office of Congressional Information and Publishing, June 8, 2012.

—. *Rare Earth Elements in National Defense: Background, Oversight Issues, and Options for Congress*, by Valerie Bailey Grasso. CRS Report R41744. Washington, DC: Office of Congressional Information and Publishing, September 17, 2013.

U.S. Nuclear Regulatory Commission. "Yellowcake Fact Sheet." http://www.nrc.gov/ reading-rm/basic-ref/glossary/yellowcake.html (accessed October 22, 2013).

"Vietnam/Japan: Vietnam, Japan Vow to Boost Rare Earth Cooperation." *Asia News Monitor* (Bangkok), July 19, 2013. ProQuest (1400734925).

"VINACOMIN and Japanese Firm to Exploit and Process Rare Earth in Lai Chau." *Vietnam National Coal-Mineral Industries Holding Corporation Limited (VINACOMIN)*, August 10, 2012. http://www.vinacomin.vn/en/news/News-and-Mining/Vinacomin-Japanese-firm-to-exploit-and-process-rare-earth-in-Lai-Chau-278.html (accessed October 17, 2013).

Wroughton, Lesley. "US, Vietnam Sign Nuclear Trade Agreement." *Reuters*, October 10, 2013. http://www.reuters.com/article/2013/10/10/us-usa-vietnam-nuclear-idUSBRE99904720131010 (accessed October 27, 2013).

Yuasa, Shino. "Rare Earth Metals Will be Mined in Vietnam by the Japanese." *The Christian Science Monitor*, October 22, 2010. http://www.csmonitor.com/World/Latest-News-Wires/2010/1022/Rare-earth-metals-will-be-mined-in-Vietnam-by-the-Japanese (accessed October 12, 2013).